# For All To Witness

## Poetry from Iraq War to DMT

# By Matthew Childers

http://www.digitalintrospect.com

**For All to Witness**
Poetry From Iraq War to DMT

---

## Introduction

The poetry in this book was written from 2003 to 2019. The poetry is not in order by the date it was written, but the earliest poems in this book were written on board a Navy amphibious assault ship on the way to Kuwait. This was less than a couple of months before I participated in the invasion of Iraq as a United States Marine Infantryman. Many of the poems in this book were written during my two deployments to Iraq.

I grew up in a small town near the city of Huntington, West Virginia. I was raised out a country road, and spent a lot of time playing outside with other kids in the neighborhood or playing video games with my little brother. By midway through high school I was getting into trouble though. I barely graduated. Not only because the amount of times I was suspended from school, but my English teacher also gave me the points I needed to pass her class. A Marine Corps recruiter got a hold of me and sold me on the dream. I wanted to travel the world, get some money to go to college, and get out of my small town. I ended up enlisting in June of 2002. To my surprise (very naive at 17) I was on a navy ship headed to the middle east just a few months after Infantry School.

I participated in two deployments to Iraq with 1st Battalion 4th Marines. The first deployment I started out as an A-gunner and then became the platoon's Designated Marksman. My second deployment I was a Fire Team Leader.

I finished my four year contract and moved to Santa Cruz, California. I moved to Oakland, California in 2010 to use the GI Bill and go to school. I now live in Oakland and work as a live visual artist and animator.

It was a struggle transitioning back to civilian life and a lot of the poetry here was inspired by that. This is self expression in the form of art. It is poetry to be specific. Nothing in this book should be taken literally. There are many things said in here that I wouldn't actually do, and there are also things said that I don't even feel anymore. Hell there are things I never felt even when I wrote it.

Thank you for accepting my invitation to witness my psycho babble in written form. I hope you find it entertaining and thought provoking. Some of it is light and fun, but a lot of it is pretty dark.

-Matthew Childers
matthew.curtis.childers@gmail.com

**They Framed Us**

Alright that's it, we're strapped in.
One hit, one toke, and we're blastin'.
-Off into outer space.
Extroverted from the human race.

I can't say we wanted it this way,
even though it was hard to relate.
Oh hell, what else can I say?
Society seems fucked off anyway.

The media says the same things
until it invades your dreams.
They control your thinking
even while you're asleep.
They've got strings on things,
and all these fucking schemes up sleeves.
They poison the water that you are drinking.

You all just think I am crazy.

Well have you thought that society made me?
You might be right but just maybe,
I won't be surprised when our world is shaking,
earth quaking, skin baking,
and they think the earth is there for the taking.
-Not on our watch!

We didn't do it. They framed us.
They put us in spiked cuffs.
They don't want us famous.
We speak truths they say are dangerous.

## Modern War Junky

As I lie on the floor,
it feels like I am falling through now.
I could pick up the pieces, sure.
but I don't wanna think about it.

I think I'll just pick up another bad habit.
Get some whiskey, beers,
and maybe some liquid acid.
Snort some coke, smoking broke.
I don't give a fuck though.

I'm in the mindset to hit the road.

If I make it alive, well there is no way to know.
The mission is top secret, destination unknown.

The rain begins to beat down.

With the stereo a psychedelic sound.
And oh you know it's on now!
These are the times when I love to live it loud.

Sounds like a time for highway nine.
I'll hug the curves in the rain.
I'll probably make it alive.
Adrenaline controls my mind.
I have to do this just so I can feel alive.

That's the way I roll.
Full throttle blast into the blown.

If I make it alive, there is no way to know.
The mission is top secret. Destination's unknown.
If I make it alive, there is no way to know.
The mission is top secret. Destination's unknown.

Tires blasting through mud holes.
The world's toughest Monte Carlo.
This is where I prefer to be.
Manifesting insanity.

Just like my friends from the USMC.
Just your average war junky.
Just a modern war junky.

They say be all that you can be!
Victimize yourself for global war profits.
Education benefits, they'll take care of it.

The money is dirty sure,
but they know you will still take it.
Suck it up and shut your mouth
there is nothing here that is sacred.

I can barely take it!
Another soul to get wasted!
But I don't wanna think about it!

I think I'll go pick up another bad habit.
Get some whiskey, beers,
and maybe some more liquid acid.
Smoking coke, smoking broke.
I don't give a fuck though.
I'm in the mindset to hit the road.

If I make it alive, well there is no way to know.
The mission is top secret
and the destinations unknown.

## My Friend

I think it's funny how things
just don't seem the same,
when I think back to the things I heard you say.

I suppose it doesn't matter.
But I still think about that disaster.
Mad Hatter. Dust in the wind.
I see you with your silly grin,
but I know of the mess your in my friend.

I hope this makes some sense.
No disrespect with this intent.
My friend.
I hope this makes some sense.
I'm just trying to be at peace with it.

I get the feeling that you've been here before.
Your lipstick smeared, drunk your on the floor.
I am too conditioned by your bullshit to be sure,
but you look at act just like a whore.

You have drool on your face,
and it's obvious you've been wasted for days.
Even from over here, I can smell your greasy vain.

You sucked me dry.
You filled me with lies
and I accepted the ride.

-I learned another lesson about this life.

No disrespect with this intent,
I am just trying to be at peace with it.
My friend.

And I hope this makes some sense,
I am just trying to be at peace with it.

My friend.

## Dirty Fingers

They stick their dirty fingers in the planet.
They planned it.
We landed to catch them candid.
Black handed.
Those who speak truth are reprimanded.

Lose citizenship in an attempt
to undermine the cruise ship.
It's sick. It's twisted. It sucks and it's fucked up.
Wait till you see how the people
are taken advantage of.

You can't patch slavery with a band-aid.
Smallpox and aids, heroin and crack to fight this.
Developed ISIS through crisis-
While Blackwater and Halliburton gets paid.

Dirty diamonds from the poor.
Not to mention Ecuador in 1994.
Door kicked to the floor by the Federal Reserve.
Run by Rapists, pedaphiles - pervs.
It's absurd. They splurge while manipulating words.

We stand for propaganda.
We cross our hearts and hope to die.
A knee taken considered sacrifice.

## Smoke, Snort, Have a Drink

As I revel in my own stink,
I sit and think, smoke, snort, then have a drink.
My legs are weak.
I get sick and puke in the kitchen sink.

A fun one who grew up a fun guy.
Abused acid, pills, crack, coke, and fungi.
Went to war to learn how greed leads people to lie,
cheat, and die.
Jokes aside when people are blown open wide.

People fall and cry to praise the sky.
Some others build a wall then stay inside.
Be afraid or die.

Get a job you hate or go to prison.
They are having a hay day
creating slaves either way.
Waiting for payday, the hard way, to fix the system.
We diss them and get eaten by the mission.

Women and children, hungry and poor,
wealthy and bored.
Healthy and pure - inhabitants of a sacred world.
Hooked on opiates is appropriate,
so they can gain our trust.
The ghettos will rust.

**Walking, Watching People Talking**

I'm downtown walking watching people talking.

11

Overhead helicopters so they can watch us.
Mega metropolis- wants to lock us up.
They see changes on their planet
and they can't stand it.

Black man blasted called bandit.
Red man with no land to land it.
No jobs to provide, we resort to do dirt or die.
The privileged question why with no perspective of
the other life.

Simple minded without the trauma to widen.
Joe Biden on private jets to Hawaii.
You can find simple words to describe me,
but the us is about to royally fuck your shit up.

We are about to fuck royalty.
Royally fuck your whole society
just to get it back where it is supposed to be.

We are dangerous and you know of us.

**Anything from Me is Yours**

Anything from me is yours.
Please disregard that all I touch is dirty,
frayed, and torn.

Everything I left,
wasn't intended to become your burden.
I'm just spilling out and on myself.

If you wouldn't mind on your way out the door,
I'd appreciate it if you would pick
my heart up off the floor.
I left it there,
but I just don't have the energy to get up.
You can take that with you too. If you want.

## People Came From All Around

People came from all around,
just so they could feel it.
The lights and sounds came from the ground
and touched everyone within it.

It rattled homes and shook souls abound,
but no one could remember what they witnessed.
Most recalled it was pleasant,
but there were moments that were wildly wicked.

They felt the race and all it's sickness.
With a smile they could see the branches
and how they're twisted.

## Moral Paradigms

When all moral paradigms are disheveled
and through the struggle even the ones closest to
you can toss a promise to oblivion.

It would appear they stand strong with a smirkish
grin and absolutely demand the mood they are in.

At moments I witness no intuition or regards
to what any other feels is happening.
Then my mind starts questioning.

What was promised and what was assumed?
What rules were broken?
Some of them must be unspoken.

People are easier to manipulate when they are
intimidated to speak. People will relate to find the
solution that they seek.
Predators prey on the weak.

But to me,
It's like pushing malevolent
thought into every empty hole,
then acting surprised when the wounds
an infection begin to grow.

How often do I stand with that
same smirkish grin feeling justified,
cutting other's answers down as if
only my own ideas can keep me occupied?

I'm not sure.

Have you ever had the intention
of attempting to witness yourself

from the outside in?
Have you ever seen a crowd
from the top row in a packed Colosseum?
It's oddly and wildly associative.

## Right Now

Looking into a mirror to see into the past,
but I see into the future
and then forget where I am at.
I take a step back, smile, and politely raise my cap.

I say,
"You and I have been together for a while."

We've each been thinking about what this means
and what we are doing-
weighing the pain we've felt
and the laughs we've had.

It's hard to say but even through the love and hate,
I am still afraid to discuss the changes to be made.

How can we see forward when I'm afraid
to tell you the places where I've been-
Even though I know you know of them.

## I Died Again

I died last night again.
Now I am existing on a different path.

For those of you who are still with me
for this particular reality,
I would like to say I'm glad you're still here too.

Remember that if anything happens to you or me,
don't worry because we will always be dancing
somewhere in the web of being.

## The Feeling That I Get

The feeling that I get is that
I should get this off my chest.
I am trying to say it best,
but first I'll have a cigarette.

The ashes on my breath.......
It's been a few nights since I've slept.......
I walk into a scrambled unknown
with a chaotic freedom I call my own.

While we are on the topic,
If I try to hurt you, I am sorry.
I thought you were trying to hurt me too.
Sometimes the reflections are too much to handle,
If you are too close
the shards can cut through you.

There was something that I said.
It doesn't matter, I forget.
I meant to feed the cats.
There are stains upon my pants.

I am guilty and obscene.
I am dirty and I'm mean.
I'll gamble all I get.
I think I'll smoke another cigarette.


## I Believe in a Freedom

I believe in freedom.
I believe in an art that is uncompromised.

I also believe in the power of the people
without the need for stained glass steeples
and public speakers masked as preachers
 to be deceitful.

Liars selling you a supposed truth
passed down for the masses to consume.
To enslave.
Those who admit that truth equals freedom
are not fearless, but brave.

Discovery can be frightening.
It can make you physically sick.
Especially if you were protecting your own ideology
only because you were raised with it.

I'd like to go without the blood stained
columns brightly lit for effect.

The stone stairs leading to a place
where the ignorant pray
and the politicians place their bets.

Mixing politics with religion is disgusting at best.

## Simple Men

"Simple men existing on a simple facade
do simple things and play simple cards.
They drop to their knees and pray to a simple god,
because simple men can't think beyond."

-God

## It's Selfish but I Can't Help It.

Right now I don't feel like learning,
I don't feel like writing, and I don't feel creative.

I want to separate from my body,
and exist entirely in a cosmic state.
For those who can relate,
I want to blow my brains into outer space.

I don't want you to talk
and I don't want to hear your voice.
I wanna be independent from input
but also with no freedom of choice.

Yeah it's selfish but I can hardly help it.

I want to exist in a limitless state.
I don't even want you to relate
because in the right light
all perception is apparently fake.

If my mind can't be meshed with infinity,
than I'd rather be in the disparity
to burn all the walls down.
You can frown and try to figure it,
but I'd rather smash every window
and dismember it.

I'd rather push the red button to turn it all around,
so real life is facing backwards,
as an entire disaster,
with all obscenities poking out.

Just for shits and shots
could everyone stand with me?
If and maybe then can I participate.
In unison let us wish it all away.
In solidarity we can pray to piss it all away.

## To The Friends Who Have Yet to Die

This is to all of my friends who have yet to die,
who dance with their steps
as reality bewilders our eyes.

The lights streak passed and they are moving fast.
Beautiful colors,
but those bumps were a little rough.
Did you hear that?
I can't get the sounds out of my head.
Up and down, through the tough shit,
and out the other side.

Do you remember the night
when we sat on the hillside,
and we all talked for hours
about whatever was on our minds?
We saw the most awesome
shooting star that night.
I am so happy we are here together
taking part in this wild ride.

We can talk shop, politics, religion and all that stuff,
or we can choose to change the world.
We can dedicate our lives to the gods,
and wage wars and conquer worlds.
It doesn't really matter either way.

We can stand outside and shout out loud
as an experiment of what it means to be alive,
or we could do the nine to five things.
It really doesn't matter.

Well I just want to say cheers, and I love you.
Let's all toss shots for the ones we have lost.
Toke it up to the token- it's a double sided coin.

## You Can Hear it Coming

You can hear it coming.
A force that will send you running
- into the woods!
You won't look back as you hear them gunning.

They want to take what is yours
when our world is flipped upside down.
We will see who is laughing now
with no ice caps and acid clouds.

The truth is the system is damned
and we can't maintain for much longer.
Too bad the illusion was stronger
than what our ancestors pondered.

Too bad the text was there too,
to tell the world to prepare,
but it was miscued by anyone who could make a
buck there.

When your laptop is a rock
they will find minerals there.
Maybe not the ancient language
that would take 3,000 years to decipher.
But maybe that's exactly how we got right here?
Another cycle around the sociatel calendar.

## Like a Mower

It's like a mower.
Mowing humans.
There is all the blood, brains,
and guts you can expect.
It's disgusting but it's the reality.
It's sick but it's true.

It's a machine.
It's got cogs
with drunken bureaucracy behind the wheel.
A bureaucracy designed
to lie, cheat, murder, and steal.
It's wildly wicked but real.

## Without This

Without this we wouldn't know what it is like.
We would take for granted all those amazing nights
where the stars were just right.

Without this hurt,
We would have never went without.
We would have never known
the magnitude of these
feelings we've allowed.

I'm going to take this time to soak in,
everything and what it is worth.
If it's worth six months of waiting
then I would give it all to make this work.

I am going to take this time to realize
what it is and what it's about.
I think it's about loving,
that feeling when you are around.

## Z

So there is a brand new designer drug
on the market called Z.
It immediately makes you insane, makes you pee,
fries your brain, gives you the sickness,
as you witness your entire life go down the drain
with a quickness.

It seizes your spine,
your teeth will grind and fall into pieces,
Your mouth leaves a trail of foam and blood
as your mind experiences telekinesis.

This is a special trip where you only get one try,
because you are guaranteed to die the first time.

Supposedly it is worth it.

## Mutated Afterbirth.

We are a disgusting
embarrassment of the universe.
A genetically tailored retarded afterbirth.
-Of what was and what will be.

A self manifested shit destiny.

Standing above the columns of a plastic civilization.
Who can help but make a mockery of this
situation?

### It's Like Magic

She wears her sigil on her chest,
engraved with ink, but laid to rest. To rot.

At best she was one of us but now fallen,
to rest with the dirt, no hurt from her nerves just
flowing-

Into the roots, and inside the redwoods,
she had dreams to accomplish but never would.

They weren't as satisfying anyway
as the shade she provides today.

### Ruby Red

My beautiful ruby red.
My life is on my hands.
Neglected by the living,
and denied to the dead.
My beautiful ruby red.

### We Can Shake it all Night

We throw our hands out and up into the sky
to thank the powers that brought together
you and I.
Every morning I witness your smile rise
under your beautiful brown eyes.
-A glimpse that gives light to the diamonds inside.

The stars are showing through all around us,
and we catch a lift just to shine.
We can shake it all night.

**Flower**

Every idea flows together.
Now and forever we continue to flower.

As long as it encompasses all
and all our will for each other,
every concept imagined will continue to prosper.

Competitiveness is fine
as long as the enemy is your brother,
That which we lean on and tether
through all the nasty weather.
Whether or not we agree all the time
or practically never,
we still want to lock arms
when the life in front of our face is severed.

Some can relate, some will debate.
Some will confuse the confusing with hate.

Some will hang their mate
over an argument's sake,
But I just like to kick around ideas
when I get drunk and baked.

Which every way you toss at night
know that all is not lost in sight,
no matter which way the coin will spin
it always ends up with hard decisions in the end.

Your blasted eyes choose to survive
and continue to grin.
Hug each other, toast the toasted,
and cheers to giving.

## Atoms and Molecules

There has got to be more to this world
 than I'm seeing.
Atoms and molecules sure,
but interdimensional beings?

You see.....perception is the key.

Just a sample of my energy,
brain chemically distorted,
and you receive a single dose of me.

## Tick Tock

With each tick of the clock, I can feel the sting,

and my mind melts with loud drips in large
cancerous drops.

Feeling distraught,
and there are others around me
who can sense the chaos.
My mask is almost lost.

The demon creeps up from underneath my skin,
and every now and again
I am not able to hold the beast in.

It rips through my grin
with intention of destruction.
It will cut anything and give infection.

It preys on the weak,
and the old,
and the different.

My body is the host.

**If You Want Me**

If you want me around why are you always gone?
If you want to build me up
then why do you kick me blue?
With every single blow
you thought I wouldn't know,
but I can see the twisted road
from which you came through.

You can bang outside and I'll wake to let you in.
I'll always greet you with a smile
to meet the same sick grief.
You've been gone a while,
and I think your liquor has a leak.
The moment your mouth opened
I could smell it stink.

With that smell
I'll taste your absolute irrational thought
and every scrap of scab
you can peel away from my old wound's clot.

Every needle you toss
toward the love that I brought
pierces me inside and out
until the holes add to a loss.

But come on in rest your head.
I'll be here in the morning.

**Chemical Oblivion**

Brains blown into a chemical oblivion.
Star spangled blood trails of a toxic psychosis.
Grinning at myself in the mirror again-
I'll never find the words
to describe the mood I'm in.

The nights are gone,

and there is no need to check my back.
I am one and all.
I've meshed with all the matter in my tracks.

To space and back with a climactic effect.
I've touched other realities, I know there is no past.

I know there is no past.
I know there is no past.

We thought we had our heads on straight.
I'd like to think it's not too late.
Although I know another way,
we drink our poisons.
Have some.

I feel the chemicals creeping in,
but we're too scared to leave our homes again.
You see the police are tweaking.

This world may seem fine to some.
But I see the world with too much wrong.
Would you like to be my baby?

Would you like to be the one who lets me down?
You seem convinced for now,
but you'll find another way out.

We drink our poisons. Have some.

**Strap Myself to a Rocket Ship**

I strap myself to a rocket ship.
I light the fuse and jet real quick.
I blast myself into the unknown and lose my soul.

Sailing forward with bright wide eyes.
Headed towards the afterlife.
I touched the stars and
then I made them my home.

All that I really know
is if I'm gonna blow a mind
it's gonna be my own.

I thumb a ride on a meteorite.
I clench my teeth as I grip real tight.
I know I shouldn't let go, but maybe I might.

Just to go to the unknown.
To a place where the truth can be shown.
I'm scared outside my head,
but at least it's my own.

All that I really know
is if I'm gonna blow a mind
it's gonna be my own.

**I've Had it**

I've had it. It's done. I'm going over.
I branch out like a tree into the sky

and look into the sun.

I would cry, but I won't without a single shoulder.
Now I'm Jumping from high boulders
just to avoid getting older.

I pray my mind to fall to pieces
and even with my weakness
I'll try harder on the weekends.
I'm reckless and senseless
out of psychological defenses
to blast myself out of all promises, contracts,
and leases.

**I Remember You**

The sorrow that beckons from within.
I remember you.

You scare me when you push so hard.
Open bleeding heart.

You are a part of me,
And the dust and foreign fragments too I suppose.
Even though it hurts to know,
I appreciate everything.

It feels good to know I feel at all.

I ride the chaos with the rest who feel lost.

I'll embrace the melding particles while
understanding the cost.

## It's Cold but I Am Cool

It's cold but I'm cool and I've been here before.
The whiskey feels warm and through all the
emotion I've endured
I just simply am who I am anymore.

Sure there are some changes I could make,
but it ain't bad anyway.
I see the stretch of space..... And we exist in it.
We feel, we breathe, we taste, we think.

It would seem we share this reality.

The trees barely sing tonight.
The moon can't even see.
The sea is too far for me
to breathe it's benevolent dreams!

The sky won't say shit,
and even though I attempt to share my plea
I have to ask,
"Why won't the stars talk to me?"

Sure I could manifest a way to mention
it in a poetic sense
but a bunch of zeros add up to nothing.
Put it down on paper and you'll see what I mean.

There are no lines you can read between.

Whenever there is an unknown
 the imagination of people
 tend to fill it with something.
Something special at that.

The darkness screams silently with pure
but wicked glee.
It offers me a taste of the absolute infinity.
Still I choose to sit. I sit and I think.
I think it's time for another drink.

I gratefully open my mouth
and stick out my tongue.
Destroying the ego is my idea of fun.
Maybe something in this drop of time
will show me the unknown.
Maybe anything and whatever. Mostly bullshit.
I'll have another drink!

If I could be lifted by the night
I would have it strip away everything.
Wash away all my pride.
It would leave me in a state
that is practically indescribable.
It demands to question everything I thought.

I've been in this position
for a few moments before,
and I can handle the fear.

I've stared over edges and
eventually jumped every time.

Leave me naked in the wind
without a sense of the honest or the wicked.
Give me a beer.
I don't need a moral code to exist.

I'll drink wildly and spin
in the cold darkness right here.
Raw and naked with no fear.

I know what's best
but my emotions get it twisted.
Hell bent and senseless
like a nasty car wreck on Christmas.

Some who claim they know
can call themselves Christian,
but this is from the one
who calls prayer glorified wishing.

**Greasy Veins**

It is the alcohol, caffeine, nicotine
and the burger king.
The onion rings, and chicken wings
for my greasy veins.
-A combination of things
that leaves my wallet empty.

## Children of the Earth

Children of the earth,
rest your heads on earthly beds.
Listen to the cosmos and listen to the winds.

The elements are not capable alone
to prove or deny a lie,
but for those who seek questions this life
like energy can certainly provide.

It's not a matter of the ultimate creation,
but how much matter can your mind contribute
towards a reasonable explanation.

As you step outside this box you realize
not many arguments make it past the typical
bluffs.

We are preprogrammed to fill in the blanks
with any other option we can think of,
but we can't accept it as truth only because you
dreamed it.

Some people will fully subscribe and die for these
manifestations. I've never understood or been able
to relate to them.

If the answers don't add up then you can deduct
that a statement saying too much with out logic is
intellectually giving up.

## Chaotic Universal Oblivion

I'm satisfied by the thought
of blowing everything I've been taught
into a chaotic universal oblivion.

I want to see all the walls come down
so I can see God again.
No boundaries or constricting ideas,
no human representation of what I should worship
- only existence for exactly what it actually is.

I want nothing to make sense
as I am determined to rinse
every human ideology and greet the other side
with a blissful kiss.

Shattering paradigms that I can only predict
will never be missed.

## This is Why you Pray

There may be no god
to judge your crooked actions,
but the law of attraction is
why you are left with what's happening.

With every intention you lie, cheat, and steal,
and you can already observe from around you that
the hell they speak of is real.

## Tramp

I glanced over to witness her trampy romance,
stopped from a prance after swinging her hip
to be stamped with a swaggy stance.

Her last ambulance ride was due to natural plants,
when refined into liquids,
providing an intravenous trance.

## It's a Gamble

A single note fills the room-
It's the most brilliant, bright blue and purple.

It's more than just a feeling
as my perceptions are conceiving
a connection graced with affection.

-Maybe a thought laced by self deception.

Although this feeling takes place in an instance
I'd call reality,
I must admit I wouldn't bet we share it.

It's a gamble with every chance I take to relate,
but I remember the days
and I beg of you to dare me.

## Too Bad

"You'll come back a changed man.
You'll do things you don't know you can."

Too bad I like the man I am.

## July 4th

Star spangled blood trails of a toxic psychosis.
You choked the constitution, fucked us,
and broke it.

And you will sing with sick sparkles in your eye,
"With bombs bursting in air",
even though you can't even contemplate war
or the kind of disgusting hate that lingers there.

You gave proof through the night
that we celebrate it-
racism, corruption, greed, and ignorance.

As you look up in the sky tonight
to solidify your wrecked reality,
just take a moment to perceive
as those who had to see-

Those who have lived under command of the
powers that be, operating with the destruction of
modern technology that was designed and
implemented to blow minds into infinity.

Pink chunks of matter
all over your sweat shop sewn designer jeans,
the whole backside of your skull
completely emptied.
Your ass is a thing of the past,
and your bodily fluids will soon be seeping.

## The Earth Replies

Another moment passes by,
as its presence splashes into the sky.
The earth trembles as the humans as why,
and what is the purpose of life.

The earth replies with a tone of demise,
"The purpose of life is to die.
A lesson to anything that questions why
is to realize these thoughts are a product
of your mind.
-Which is the ultimate goal of sustaining your life."

As the wind blows dead leaves across my achy feet,
I can smell the death in the air.
As I inhale I realize that
these could be my last seconds
 of being able to care.

All I know of this mystery
is its complexities fascinate me.
And if on my way home I happen to die,

I am just grateful I had the opportunity to be alive.

## Organize Your Dreams

Organize your dreams,
then pack them up and run with me,
because I've got a feeling we are running in the
same direction.

I've got a feeling we will reach our destination.
All you needed was a companion,
and I am here to make it happen.

## A Single Note

A single note tones the room.
It's infinite.
I see nothing.
I feel nothing.

Waiting for a change of pulse
 to tune my heart felt strings.
It's depriving, not surprising,
as I drift across seas.

Callused as my brain,
my hands reach towards the drain.
Skin becomes stained with blood
as I declot these foreign thoughts.

It breaks apart in a sour mess.

I just wipe it on my chest.

## Sing With Me

Silence would be comforting
if it wasn't so thick and heavy,
-laying on my chest
with the weight against my breath.

Give me a rhythm to lighten this load.
Give me those inspirations my heart will know.
Carry a melody for the world.
Sing with me, Sing with me.

Darkness tastes like a certain nothing inside my
soul.
Stale mixed with stagnant sorrow takes the
control.

Give me your life to color this day.
Something to move to and take me away.
Give me your beauty with those words you sing.
Sing with me, Sing with me.

## James Blames Himself

It seemed like we were on the same page
a few years ago,
but now things have changed
since James can think on his own.

"It's obscene and disgusting to me
to think that I could fall subject
to your brainwashing.
But now here I am,
questioning my reason for escaping fatality
when I deserved to die just as well as the next guy.

Well I took part in your political war,
and did everything you could ask for.
And just so you know, I believe in every aspect
that you took advantage of me.

I am not going to say you made me do it,
or that you put a gun to my head,
but you put one in my hand,
and gave me the option of death instead."

James doesn't know who to blame,
so he blames himself today.

**Becoming Stale**

Everything is becoming stale,
tasteless in its own sense,
in concrete but still incomplete.
Wondering how much longer I can drift like this.

I can no longer say that what I am feeling is pain,
but more like all emotions run in the same.
More like I am losing and tired of this game.
-Too tired to feel sore or anything but bored.

The seconds will turn to minutes,
and then soon to a year,
but it's too difficult to see the light right now.

## Pawns

Change my mindset for 6 months.
Give me an order so I can bite my tongue.
After all, I chose this fate,
to start my life on a brand new slate.

Sad to say I have become the authority
representing everything I hate.
But I won't adjust my personality.
Just hold it off to a later day.

Mold your slaves to fight your wars,
their mental states will be ignored.
To trust these people with our lives?
I'll trust no one with my life.

We are only pawns to them,
just game pieces so they can win
these wars of pride they have fought for years,
while Jesus and Muhammad shed their tears.

## It's Dark Again
It is a brand new day,
but it is dark again.
Stuck, broke, and out of luck.

I am in no mood to force a grin.

The walls have closed in,
the tightness in my chest makes it hard to breathe,
no longer can I speak,
I grab some weed for some instant relief.

My pupils feel dry
as I've been crying for some time.
My nerves tense to accelerate
the pace of my mind.

How long has this been going on?
For years now I would say the least.
It seems as if I've always been wrong.
I'm beginning to admit my defeat.

Then again I finish my reach,
for the bottle and the lighter to spark relief.
Anything and everything to set my mind at peace.
Maybe tonight I will manage to sleep.

**Beautiful Smile**

It was all of the little things
I consistently took for granted,
and they still come back to me on a daily basis.
The other day when I walked away,
a frame of feeling flashed through my mind.

It was as if no time had passed since last year
when I would come home to your beautiful smile.

## Time Doesn't Exist.

The future is right now,
and our pasts are present today.
Seconds are merely a tool,
for human beings to relate.

But none of it is true.
I promise you that time does not exist.
We are so advanced,
we can't recognize our own ignorance.

The sun rises and falls,
and we call it a day when it ends.
But things might look different
from the outside looking in.

Fortunately we don't live forever,
and humans do become old and die.
But we become dead in the now,
as our molecular structure falls from its binds.

## When Do You Think They Will Drop the Bomb?

Reality has lost all sensibility
here in my world of constant fatigue,
anxiety, and the undenying perception of mortality.

"When do you think they will drop the bomb?"

## Can You Remember?

You seemed on the verge of having a good time,
Until you realized your life
was being held on the line.

Until you realized that everything
you know and love isn't guaranteed,
and simplicity doesn't describe
your faith up above.

Well this could be the point,
and this could the moment,
the instant when you realize
that fate isn't absent.

Can you remember everything
that changed your state of mind?
Made you who you are everyday up until this time?
Because this could be it forever.
I hope we can stay together,
but promises would be pointless
and coming from a state of ignorance.

Wishing I could look ahead
to maybe get a feeling of comfort.
It's an uneasy feeling knowing
these could be my last seconds of breathing.

## Never Have I Ever

Never have I walked so far for anything.
My whole life has changed
over one decision I've made.
I am thousands of miles away from that day
without an option to trade.
Thousands of miles away
without one regret to say.
No doubt my life has changed.
This is life or death, win or lose,
with nothing in between.
There is still more to this world to be seen.
I'll walk a thousand more miles just to succeed.
I will go on until my fucking soul bleeds.

## No One Gives a Fuck

Your life is dissolved, and your mind is dust.
Your words are lies, and your feelings are mush.
Grab your nuts and suck it up.
You must realize that no one gives a fuck.

## Here I am Lost

Can't find a song to match the mood I'm in,
and I am afraid my mind is going to wander again.

I am afraid there is nothing left to do.
If only I had the chance to talk to you.

These roads are dark
and the wind blows dead leaves across my path.
The night silently whispers the need to check my
back.

## Losing Something

I feel like I am losing something.
It feels like it's fading somewhere out of reach.
It doesn't matter how much I struggle
because  nothing in my power
can bring you any closer.
Is it that time already?  Can't you wait until January?
It's a torment that ricochets inside
the center of my mind,
and I know it sounds so cliche
but all we have is time.

It's probably all in my head in the first place,
but it would be a shame to put this ink to waste.

Be ashamed and help me with this bitter taste.
If I could only get through these sound proof walls I
could fix this situation.
I guess I have found my letter long fixation.

## They Call Upon Their Gods

They call upon their gods at night,
and they make sure we can hear.
The vibrating tones excite my spine

once they have left my ear.

The sound of hope for them
is the sound of death for me.
But the skies and streets are black,
and my field of vision is green.

A bead of sweat collects with the rest
and the salt stings my eyes,
But no discomfort can match
the pain that's in my mind.

Stomach is churning while bodies are burning,
Will I make it another day?

My hands are red.
My friends are dead.
And it's all in Jesus and Muhammad's name.

Only a photograph in my pocket keeps me
grounded at this time.
Only a desire to live keeps me
fighting on their side.

**TRAPPED**

Trapped!
Small white room,
one window, and no curtains.
Running short of air,
and boredom is certain.

"We are almost out of luck."
Like a man, and true spoken.
"Set aside all pleasurable things.
We are the few chosen."

Thoughts going dry.
What is left to say?
"Please wait a little longer.
I will be back someday"

Exhausted, lonely, anxious, angry.
Keep your pen moving.
Your words can save me.

Sorrow, boredom, stale, exhale.
-Keep in mind it's not forever.
Not here in my white room cell

## Chemically Induced

Chemically induced by substances
my brain didn't produce.
-Even though the receptors are there,
to view reality through pupils that care.

## Can't Sleep?

Can't sleep?
Take a deep breath.
Hold it in,

but don't strain yourself yet.
As you exhale,
dream of thoughts so gentle.

Feeling the comfort ease under your eyes,
as alive as you are, you are not there yet.
Don't dream too far.

Remember the way her skin felt?
Soft and warm with every second adorn?
You may kiss her bare shoulders as she sleeps.

Speckled brown works of beautiful body.
You may tell her you love her as she sleeps.

Her dark hair across her pretty face.
Laying in blankets your mind dazed with her grace.
-Knowing your heart has found its place.

Rest assured knowing hers has too.
Dreaming these thoughts only with you.

**The Fist**

Where is your pride now?
You swallowed it with a fist.
Brush it off like you don't care,
but I can see what you won't admit.

She looks towards you for protection.
Her thoughts are a misconception.

Walking through mirrors,
avoiding your own reflection.

The ground becomes more appealing
as your weakness is more revealing.
There isn't much inside
to make it worth concealing.

Bite your lip and clench your fists.
Dry your eyes and deal with it.
Let yourself wash away.
The fist is here to stay.

## Symmetric Binary Tree

It's represented by our foot paths.
It carves our rivers and our caves.
It's pattern is represented
by the nerves in our brains,
and our blood that flows through
the route of our veins.
It maybe the absence of design.
And randomness in it's true sense.

## Which Way?

Which road should I take?
Which hole as a grave?
Decisions ahead.
Which ones should I make?

Would I be submitting myself
to the teeth of the system,
if I want a family, and the money to raise them?

If they have me with a hook,
then I am sure it's love, and maybe a spirit,
or something above.

Either way I've already fallen to the jaws.
And why complain?
Comfort feels good after all.

## I've Found the Answer!

I've found the answer!
It's like slowly falling.
Just enough to pace your breath,
with a humming sensation in your chest.

Blanketed by warmth,
Now comfortably floating.
Overwhelmed with bliss,
and a sense of belonging.

My God I have found the answer!

Now I can live in peace.
This void has been fulfilled.
I can walk upon my feet.

I love you.

## I Look Inside

I look inside.
All I can find is a dirty rag knotted with lies.
I know that you can't find me,
so I guess I'll find myself.
I'll put mistakes behind me.
You'll save them for yourself.

I could go clean, but it's probably too late.
I never meant to deceive.
I fall to my knees so,
I can manage to sleep.
I wish somebody could save me.

## You Can See the Blood

You can see fresh blood on the stone
if you look through the indoctrination.
You can even hear the cries of the dead
to smash the senate's face in.

Standing below the columns of colonization
noticing the funding we provide to paint their
perfect image.

If you cast the right shadows
you can create a position.
-A position to hide, mask lies, and disregard lives.

I could see the blood on the walls,
but I felt her love even more.
It gave me hope that the population
is growing ready,
and someday we will burn this system
to the fucking floor.

## I Wanna Be Alone

Turn the lights out.
Shut the door now.
Turn around and walk away from my house.

If you see me out,
please turn around.
I don't want to share my thoughts with you.

I wanna be alone.
I wanna be alone.

With the shades down,
and the lights drown out.
Ideas come about and seize
the words from my mouth.

So you're feeling proud.
You love to run your mouth.
Nothing I care about.
I've told you once I wanna be alone.
I wanna be alone.

If you see me dancing in outer space,
have the courtesy to walk away.

Pull the mask from over my eyes.
Five bucks a hit for the expansion of my mind.

My psyche is spiraling round.
My soul smashed through the ground.
Consciousness drowning out,
and I don't give a fuck about it.

I wanna be alone.
I wanna be alone.

## You Can't Change me.

I know what I want.
I know what I need.
And no, I can't find it here.

I know what I see.
I know what I think,
and you can't change me.

You can lead me around here
with your stupid games,
But you can't get the best of me.
You don't realize, I am not in your army.
I still have my head. I am still free.

Mindless brainwashed lack of soul.

Understand when I say no.
And I'm sorry that I hurt your pride.
There is more to me than meets the eye.

## Let Me Out!

Let me out!
I can't get away from these sounds.
Left, Right, Left, Right.
Heels driving into the ground.


Surrounded by ignorance.
Doing things the hard way.
Psychopaths writing screen plays,
singing "Waste em' all away!"

"Blood, Guts, Kill, Repeat"
"Blood, Guts, Kill, Repeat"

## Swimming Through Muddy Water

Swimming through muddy water,
I'll raise my head for just a breath.
Smash my face into glass.
Everything cuts me anyway.

Choking on your falling ashes.
I haven't burned out yet.
Blood still remains within my veins.
It's only stagnant.

I am doing just fine.

The rain still pours and we are both wet,
but I am dry inside.
As you witness my legs are bloody,
but my jeans have no rips.

Crashing through your brilliance
with no desire to stop yet.
Pavement hurts and my mind jerks,
but I am not dead yet.

If I could destroy emotion,
I still wouldn't reconsider.
You laid it out soaked in my shit,
and I remain to lie in it.

With a smiling face my eyes go blank
and my teeth begin to grind.
It's your cold shoulder that kills the moon
and sends shivers down my spine.

**I'm Moving On**

The weather is changing, and honey so am I.
I'm not gonna open any more wounds for you.
There is no time to die.

No safe direction.
No place to hide.
But I'm running over mountains babe.

I'm leaving nothing behind.

Well, I thought I would tell you
that I am moving on.

The wind still howls for me.
The waves crash on the sand.
I don't need a crutch for anything,
except the spliff in my hand.

There is no telling where I will be
or who I will be with,
but my face and clothes are clean,
and I'm stealing a kiss.

I thought I would tell you, I'm moving on.
No more messing with me. I'm moving on.

## Standing on the Edge

Standing on the edge of sanity
with a billion stars stretched across my face.
Riddling my eyes- reminds me of my impurities,
disgust, and heartfelt distaste.

Which option to take?
Which hole as a grave?
Which rules do I bend?
Which rules do I break?

Wherever you lay your head

my heart is not far away.
The souls we've meshed have withstood tests,
and the binding is tightly laced.

Hands conjoined with fingers interlaced.
The energy of your presence radiates
through my mind,
down my spine,
and opens my eyes as a reflection of yours.

You are a spectrum of natural beauty,
and a symbol of the beauty of humanity.
We thank the universe for your existence,
and we praise the powers that join us.

**Sick and Twisted**

Sick and twisted,
hell bent and deliberate
with a cocked smile and raised brow
promising hell forever and now.

They stand above the crowd,
looking down, declaring how.
Blood all around and bodies inside out.
People screaming in all directions
running over each other on the ground.

As if this conflict was a joke
cast on the asses of all the ignorant.
The masses of the disillusioned

fabricated the descent
of the american flag
and all that stands with it.

As if it's a fact that was proclaimed by the authority
who are absolutely malevolent.
The media twists our words so hard
there can be nothing left relevant.

We keep going in the same full circle,
until someone rips the cycle down
and tops the temple over.

As if most of us can imagine how
the justice system ended up upside down.
They say some souls were destined for torture
and cast out into the hells for eternity
since to you and me this random worships
a foreign entity.

Peace for each being throwing their hands up
in the air to declare their love for humanity.

Not the back washed distorted version of Jesus
Christ that you wave around proudly,
even though you've contorted a message
you did not write.

## Chasing Her Supernova

Another glimpse into infinity.

Chasing this spiritual butterfly into her supernova.
She is aware of the thoughts I toss over.

## Damn Us All and Damn Our Maker

As you reach into the sky,
dreaming only as the dreamers try,
shield your eyes, and take some shelter.
It's our existence that compels her.

Even if it's nuclear war, it's mother nature.
Damn us all and damn our maker.

Damn us all and damn our creator.
It wasn't her that made me hate her.
My judgement is ruled by emotions,
I can't control my anger.
These things make more sense on paper.

She says I'm out of control, and I don't blame her
It wasn't her that made me hate her.
Damn us all and damn our maker.

## Poison in My Veins

The thought again.
The rising pulse.
Waiting for what I love the most.
Staring into a plastic sky.
Reflecting the image of a plastic guy.

My direction has changed with the wind.
Trying to find that song again.
What's for tomorrow? Cloudy Skies?
Cover me while I choose to lie.

Mask my movement, test my involvement.
Poison in my veins, Poison in my veins.

Fulfillment can not be found in this chair,
Poison in my veins, Poison in my veins.

## There is Something in Sync

There is something in sync
that exists with every blink.
It's there with every thought that you think,
and amidst all the chaos that's happening.

It's more than the words
that I can scribble on bar napkins.

The beauty of it all is every possible conceived
ideology that one can present is most certainly
wrong.

Even the ones I cherish and have sworn by the
night they are right all along.

It's as if we are flawed-
sociologically discouraged
and disconnected from

that in which we are nourished.

There are space bound radicals
attracted to fractals and cosmic paths,
Plutocracy enabled tyrannical
 who preach fears of god's wrath
- and every other stereotype
 that falls within the cracks.

Regardless of your ego, in fact
we live in a codependent habitat,
where every species has taken its path
to manifest the human race.

Regardless of your feelings for not believing,
this species has been united
to create everything you are seeing.

Just another habitual abstraction that manifests
from a collection of perceived answers,
but even considering all of the fear and the hate,
you wouldn't be here
if you hadn't found a way to relate.

We're merely prayers.
Just players in a universal roll of the dice.

It's like particles sliced into sub particles
- in half again -in half again, and every time it's like
observing everything from the absolute beginning.

Some say we can only contemplate
what we are seeing,
but they forget that the act of dreaming
might as well be reality in the moment that the
being is experiencing.

Are you dreaming?
It's like as long as we look
there is something to find.

Either way there is something in sync
that exists with every blink.
It's there with every thought that you think,
and amidst all the chaos that's happening.

It's more than the words
that I can scribble on bar napkins.

## A Curse

It's hollow, bland, ugly, broken,
degenerated, disgusting, devolved, and discerning.

It lurks in every face and eyeball,
and every hole that you believe contains a soul.

Every pore equipped with a spinal cord
suddenly has wings in the disillusioned and the
obviously bored.

–but your actions show none of that and much
more.

... As if you live in the past
with your mind just as dust
as the ass of the revolutionaries who spoke
on the cusp and the birth of this planet
we call earth.

It's a curse disguised with a cross and a mask.

## Still Not Good Enough

I poured myself out and all over myself.
I lie in a puddle, in trouble, and empty.
It is simply because I can't figure out
why I am doing this really.

I don't think I was born with the guts
to make the cut,
and the one thing I am good at
I am still not good enough.
If I could catch a mood to lift me up
please someone lift me out of this rut.

## Ben Dover

You always knew I was a passionate fool,
but you fucked me over anyways
and broke your own rules.

Now you've got a monster on your back,
and I'll cut no slack, but I will cut your throat.
Fucker.

But not like you hoped.......
this will take far more time and energy,
but it's worth every drip.

You'll know that and exactly what you should,
and you owe me with every blow to your psyche.

When you screwed me
you gave birth to your own demons
who have been riding behind your fake smile
obviously for quite a while.

You cursed the earth with the visions
you are perceiving,
and my mouth is frothy with your blood.

Count your blessings and say your prayers fucker.
You'll need the Mother Mary
like you never thought you would.

## Scam Artist at Best

I barely saw your shadow standing there
with its hands behind your back.
But you both wear the exact same glare,
and the same grin that will bite your ass.

Some call you a magician,
but you fail to manifest.
Just a scam artist at best
with a strange sigil on your chest.

You lie, you cheat, and you steal.
I desire to find a way to hurt you
to prove that you can feel.

## Demons at My Feet

I will gamble all I get. I will smoke a cigarette.
There is always a need. I need to be set free.
The demons have been in the sheets while I sleep.
While these thoughts are in my head
and I wish that I was dead.

I get away instead. I smoke a cigarette.
I gamble all I earn,
and I smoke much more than that!

## Don't Drink and Drive

I am driving highways,
going sideways, high on three j's,
I always make it- even naked.
I get wasted. You can taste it.

I used to be invisible. Now I am invincible.
Now loud still critical.
Silly fool who breaks the rules.

You can't lose without the rules.

Ride the rails like I am going off em.
Escaping jail fairly often.
I think we lost them.
Sound has softened.
The way I clown could put me in a coffin.

They chase me down.
I back up off em'.
Light the gas, and blast off laughing.
Distracted misshapen, disastrous,
instantaneous, spazmatic-
mad hatter, no better,
so clever, pervert.

Nerves hurt, side jerk,
nervous twitch.
Turns out I am now inside out
waking up in a ditch.
What a bitch.

The lesson is don't drink and drive kids.

**Vampire**

I was hypnotized,
and I barely noticed the fangs
before it was too late.
Through all the time she spent with me,
I hadn't realized it was only so she could feed.

At last she revealed the fangs
with a brazen display,
because she thought she had me
under her wing.
But you see I broke from my trance
and was ready to flee.

Luckily I got away but everytime I blink,
I can see her grin covered with blood
she got from me then.

## Remembering Those Gifts They Brought.

We celebrate with open hugs
with love to all above.
They had to miss it, mixed through twisted,
but at least we are together and now still feeling
blessed and gifted.

We've seen them go, we take a shot,
we thank the gods that made them rot.
We thank them all, the big and small,
remembering those gifts they brought.

The afterthought can be unbearing,
to recognize the universe is so scary.
But with wide eyes and an eager grin
we step into the unknown again.

## Moving On Again

Last time I held you in my arms,
I knew it might be it before you went moving on.
I held you tight while you were sleeping,
and made a point to cherish the moment
while listening to your breathing.

Now I drive alone with the breeze
by hills and trees.
I can't help but remember what it was like
when you were here next to me.

Moving on into the unknown
with secrets you'll never know.
I hope you understand it's true
that I will always love you.

## Lose Your Grip

Lose your grip and fall back gasping
into a pattern of relapsing events.
It's intended from birth to dissonance.

The boots march to cadence
with parts of the mechanics,
-twisting, turning, grinding
and burning for survival.

It can be heaven and hell
with no preference in disparity.
There is no moral code
when looking at things objectively.

God and all and the insects within the walls.
They loot, they prey, they fuck, and they kill.
 -But maybe the more complex the ecosystem
the greater the will.

It's as if it's built into the code of life,
to rise from the reptilians
 for the sake of our organics.

To shed ignorance like a skin
if it means technology can erase original sin.

Adam and Eve were destined to bring alternate
energy through computer mathematics.

Our only human purpose was to save the earth.

**Blood Bubbles**

Blood bubbles, pink fragments, fat, muscle,
and a glimpse of bone.
Gasping struggle, mashed into rubble,
concrete through your ass,
car crashed and in trouble.

I mumbled and stumbled
as I used her phone to call for help.
To me it looked as if her intestines were falling out.
A couple came from across the street,
but when they saw

one immediately puked and fell.

Get us out of this hell!

It is upside down now.
I can see inside your body.
God don't rob us of her life!
Please baby tell me that you love me!

## Demons

The experience unfolding
into a bewildering unknown,
With a past that is dirty
cradling the wicked to be shown.

The present is hard to live in
when I am terrified to explore.
Those demons, they are creeping,
with one direction, out of holes.

I hear them walking,
I hear them whispering through my phone.
I hear knocking
 and decide to let them in my home.

## Punch Drunk

Your punch is to be drunken of.
Our lunch was to be given up.
The gods needed a better taste of you.

Now they wild in your glory.
It is young and it's pouring.
The sun is showing its mourning,
and I am left with only a story.

## Fuck If Love Only Made Sense

I never liked it when you were so wasted.
I was burnt out and feeling jaded.
Makes me think we could of made it,
But I'd be burnt out and feeling jaded.

Your laugh was so sweet,
but that scowl went with your sours.
No need to ask If you'd compromise that power.
-We wouldn't have made it an hour my flower!

It took me so long to give you up,
and sometimes I still feel like diving back in.
-To pick up again with all the gin in the end,
With the yelling and screaming,
and walking on ceilings,
losing my hair, and falling downstairs- it's intense!

-Fuck, if love only made sense.

## Clean Cut, but Loosened Up.

Clean cut, but loosened up.
Three hits deep - light on my feet.

Eyes wide and blinging.
Total geek but scorpion stinging.

Twisted and dreaming!
Relaxing while deeming!
Talking to aliens while they show me their city.

It's so pretty,
and they gave me a message
but no one can read it.
It is up to you and me to translate.

Never fake it.
Homosapien naked.
Take my soul and rearrange it.
Give it back to the planet.

## You Move so Slow

It maybe because you move so slow.
There is something in sync,
I watch your lips moving and it makes me smile.

I am not sure what you said,
but I know I like it.
I can chill just like this for a while.

Your brown skin next to mine-
I can chill like this all the time.
We can fly with the wind,
so I can watch you in your flow.

You know I love you so.

## Giving a Fuck of

I hope you are not saying things
just so you can say them.
Look me in the eyes and say it again.
I can see your soul my friend.

Look into me please. I am begging you.
I am raw, naked, and opened
up just for you to stir me up.

Tell me exactly what you are thinking of.

## Living Wild

It's good to see you living wild.
I can see the weather in your eyes.
I love that you have questioned all-
most would shut the door to stay inside.

I love that you have made your own path.
We can only attempt to follow
the tracks you've left.

Even though you express doubt with it,
I love exactly where you are at.

## A Million Snakes

A million snakes lick our skin,
And it is freezing smooth.
The night winds sing for us,
And the redwoods hide the moon.

The sky says it's on our side
and wishes to take us on a ride.
Once we commit it is do or die,
No room to compromise.

Look me in the eyes and tell me your mission.
The snakes, the trees, frogs, and the breeze
are all listening just to witness.

Are you willing to risk everything
for the chance to grow our wings?
Are you willing to fly with me into the sky
and gamble what the future brings?

**Bye**

I ran too far and got lost from home.
No excuses no.
I guess I just had to see how it could happen.
I looked over the edge
and the anxiety had me gasping.

I promised myself
I would never let fear become a distraction.
I was just about to jump when you shoved me.

It is a long fall, and I can't hear or see you anymore.

Sometimes it's very cold and dark.
Sometimes the sun shines bright
and it feels good on my skin.
Sometimes I feel dead,
but sometimes I feel brand new again.
I guess this is the end.
I wish you the best my friend.

## One Time

I met this dude one time.
He reminded me so much of my dear friend
who had died.
I tried to forget it and get lost in conversation,
but it tripped me out all night.

He looked a lot like him,
and shared some of the same mannerisms too.
He needed a place to stay for the night,
so I allowed him to come through.

We talked and indulged in K
for a few an hour or two.
The eeriness began to haunt me in a way,
and eventually I had to tell him the truth.

He acted as if it was no surprise,
because a few years ago he almost lost his life.

He continued to reply,

"Ever since that day,
I have always felt like I am someone else.
And you seem oddly familiar yourself.
Tell me more about Johnny."

     - I never mentioned his name.

## The Wind Blows

You must have mistaken me
as a leaf from the trees
with no recognition of where the wind blows
or what the branches whispered.

The world isn't made up of all you can picture.
I hear the words,
but we'd like to invite you to see the bigger picture.

## Manipulating Forces

Manipulating forces take truth, fuck you,
then they hold it and contort it.
They take fortunes
-no regards to other class, sex or race,

- for or against the abortions....
You look for solutions by pointing a middle finger
towards those who you were taught to.
Ironically it's a hate you weren't born with.
It's a catch 22 and we lose dude.

I'm not a contortionist,
but my body is here
to go through all of the motions.
Just tell me how to relate
- and I'll move in ways to display
all the hate you say.

**Tick**

The next time you see me in public
I will be walking up to you
with pleasure in my eyes and a crooked grin.
As I come face to face with you again
You'll hear me whisper,

"I hope you wake up screaming every single night
from the nightmares of your guilty conciseness
you are damned to possess. I hope you scream so
loud it hurts your chest, as these words that stab
your spine come equipped with a hex."

You are a tick
and you got within reach of some good blood.
I can see you got swollen and filled up,
but there is a river where this blood comes from.

You can't handle the sip,
because I will smash your fat ass
and all your wickedness.

I hope it was worth every drip
you dumb swollen ugly blood sucking tick.

## The Fuck Holes

The fuck holes. They can fuck you.
They can trick you to think- "FUCK!"
Those fuck holes,
 you know they can fuck a hole,
or absolutely anything.

Watch that fuck head as they fuck hole.

## Dead End

I can perceive the message you cast out to me.
Through the twigs and the wilted leaves,
you know I can see.
I believe you know how to speak the truth to me.

I think I can too.
At once we could deceive.
I know we both did.

That was until we could see each other as mirrors
and fragments and had the chance to make sense
of all that madness that has happened.

We got to this dead end.
I think it takes space sometimes
to gather our perception.

Regardless of the shards
and the shrapnel that we've witnessed,
I wouldn't take back anything
-especially the emotion felt since then.

And to think it may have happened for a reason.

**Walking Me**

I feel like this walk is walking me.
I'm like a dog on a leash-
Foaming mouth, but set me free.
Weak knees, I'm displeased with all I see.
Like I've got a strange disease,
hanging shady under trees with sharp ass teeth,
and I beg for cures from strangers.
Pretty please!

**Welcome To Our Party**

Take that floating thought. Grab it, hold it.
Turn it inside out. Shape it, mold it.

Tell us all out loud.
We would never be ashamed.

Welcome to our party!
We built it just for everyone.
You are allowed to cry.
Please don't mind if we hug you.

Some of us will go away,
and that will be okay too.
Through all the tears we will end with a smile. ☐

Every time you are down
we will help you back around.

Welcome to our celebration!

It's wild but pure,
and even with all the discomfort
we've allured together,
I'm still beyond thrilled we can hold each other.

This gift of life is something else.
Thank you for sharing your special self.

## Beautiful Disaster

The lights and sounds argue outside.
They are yellow, loud, and angry.
I waited for a red light,
but it was too late by the time I saw it.

My friends like to poke and taunt,
just to disrupt a thought for some attention.
Sometimes I need to search hard for a space
to call all mine even if it wasn't my initial intention.

These thoughts wanna be free to come and go
without the persistent thought control.

Without another reaching over
to grab my soul and pull me closer.

Demand another wish from me
and I'll cast away into it all
-where my peace and stars are all in all,
casually watching over
the casual demanding from each other.

Large masses of heads and arms
all moving in unique ways,
but still projecting a pattern.
It seems random at first
but the algorithm shows itself
when you pull back a bit.

Watching from the outside, I feel like it all,
and I can imagine the mass destruction
that could happen.

 - A giant blender murdering
 to whip all social classes.
It's sick and twisted,
but I can imagine if it happened.

I see the mower move forward
to blend sugar infused masses into molasses.
Mothers stand back disgusted and gasping,
watching nature choose which lives are saved
or considered a hazard.

A kind of beautiful disaster.

## Wild World

This world is wild. It's beautiful and it's terrifying.
I can mostly smile at the spirit
even when it shakes me.

I'll allow it to take me for a ride
for as long as it needs to teach me.
I'll laugh and cry at times along the way,
but even the tears can feed.

It hurts to grow
and accomplishment is met with another struggle.
We dig deep for surprise within this rubble.

## Dynamite Car Crash

My bones are in my body.... I can feel them there.
Your eyes are on the back of my mind.
I can feel your glare.

Brown hair,
speckled beautiful body blown into an oblivion.

Memories of the dynamite disaster
car crash again.

## Just Say I Chose

I believe in both.
You could toss a coin and say I chose.
To believe like I cast it all into the unknown....

A benevolent blown into cosmos.
I choke on the dust we arose
and then smoke holes through
the thoughts that evoke you.

I can care less as long as I know that you do too.

**Fuck shit up**

I want to cry. I want to cuss.
I want to scream out loud and fuck shit up.
Disgust through my veins and It's all fucked up.
I want to burn. I want to thrill.
Instead I think I'll sit right here.
Drink in one hand and smoke in another.

-Staring through dimensions
as if I could be another.
Star crossed lovers
blown to bits by fragments of shit.

If this was the second time
I might not yet be sick of it.

Change my mind to the way it was another time.
The clock chimes and stabs me in the head again.

Feeling like I'd rather be dead instead,
my big head caused me to have bled my friend.

As if today wasn't bad it's tomorrow I dread.

## Something Strange

If you breathe, you can grieve,
you can cry, and you can bleed.
If you need, you'll get hexed.
We escape to dance with wickedness.

The trees and moon are blessed.
I can feel something in my chest.
Summoning demons with tribal beats
to be released.

We move our feet,
the purge of demons beneath.
We were scarred to move urgently.

Remove disease from my mind pretty please!
My eyeballs are molded green,
and there is something strange living in between.
I am hallucinating the most crazy shit
I have ever seen.

I can hear the dark side there
waiting and calling me.
I try to hide and plead,
but there is no escaping me.

I might as well listen.
The dark has chosen me.

## Twin Peaks Inn

The walls are yellow brown.
Ugly sounds bounce all around.
Blood stains, alcohol and coffee.
I stop next door for a white Russian-
stubbed my toe once and never stopped cussing.

I almost bumped into that man
and I thought he might rob me.
Immediately after another one got to close
when asking me for a cigarette.

He said he was trying to get high like me,
but I couldn't tell what he was getting at.
I had no idea what
he was trying to get off his chest.
But as I walked away he mumbled something
about sucking cock the best.

The bartender is smooth
and he likes to tell me stories.
He tells me about him and his gay uncle drinking
white Russians in Vegas.

He said after so many his uncle would get horny,
and he was sure to be in
the male strip clubs by morning.

They called the routine morning glory.

I think I'll have one more drink
before heading back to my room
to have two more drinks.
At that point I'll like the way I think and then sleep.

## Ideas Conjunctive Juxtaposed

Sometimes we make a deliberate choice
to look into our past,
and sometimes it hurts too much to go further.

Through all the nightmares, traumas, and various
lovers I would still rather be myself than any other.
I can put two feet down
and manage to speak my thoughts out loud,
even if there is no other to hear
the garble and rubble.

It's honestly mostly gibberish,
but if you can make decent sense of it,
then we relate enough for me
to call you my brother.

At some points I'll toss many coins into oblivion...
into ponds, lakes, and fountains.
With a silly grin, I'll do my best to test superstition
and the world we live in.

|Is material matter? Do I have what they're after?

Are we content with disaster while the puppets fill
their pockets with money in fits of mad laughter?

We all live our own lives I suppose.
Although the choices are seemingly infinite they
become more conjunctive juxtaposed.

## He Knows

She writes him letters almost everyday.
It's been about four months
since he has been away.

Clinging on to the things that he left her,
in remembrance of the times together.

All they can do is dream and think,
but he knows one promise he can't guarantee.

## Manic on Acid

It's a manic on acid.  A psychologist's orgasm.
It's a violent pornography.
Product of a violent history.

It's the wars that pave our streets.
It's the shoes upon our feet.
We think we own the planet.
 -Guaranteed our own enslavement.

Another bullshit transmission
of reality molestation.
We fall upon our knees
in an attempt to cry our minds to peace.

Substance abuse provides a comforting delirium,
so I can find some peace inside the room
I'm spinning in.

I'm sure we will never be the same again,
but that is the reality that we are living in.

It might as well be over,
so raise a glass and say cheers,
and thank the universe
for our last blasphemous years.

Thank the media for controlling our fears.
Thank the gasoline
so we can live American dreams.

Thank Mexico,
for for staying the fuck out of my shit!

Is anyone else here getting sick of this?

**It's Tough to Lose a Friend.**

There are so many things
I wish I could have done or said.
There is evidence of his existence all around me.

-Trails Of objects and nic-nacs  connected to my memory.


 I can't believe he is gone.

I send my thoughts into the cosmos
wishing for a reply,

 "Thanks again for all of the wonderful times."

Made in the USA
Las Vegas, NV
06 May 2022

48467355R10059